Faustina Kowalska

Blessed Are the Merciful

1905–1938

Born in Głogowiec, Poland

Feast Day: October 5

Patron of Mercy

"Blessed are the merciful,
for they will be shown mercy."
Matthew 5:7

Text by Barbara Yoffie
Illustrated by Chris Sharp

Liguori Publications
A Redemptorist Ministry

Dedication

To my family:
my parents Jim and Peg,
my husband Bill,
our son Sam and daughter-in-law Erin,
and our precious grandchildren
Ben, Lucas, and Andrew

To all the children I have had the privilege of teaching throughout the years.

Imprimi Potest:
Kevin Zubel, CSsR, Provincial
Denver Province, the Redemptorists

Published by Liguori Publications, Liguori, Missouri 63057
To order, visit Liguori.org or call 800-325-9521.

ISBN (print): 978-0-7648-2879-9
ISBN (digital): 978-0-7648-2774-0

Liguori Publications, a nonprofit corporation, is an apostolate of the Redemptorists. To learn more about the Redemptorists, visit Redemptorists.com.

Printed in the United States of America
27 26 25 24 23 / 5 4 3 2 1
First Edition

Dear Parents and Teachers:

Saints and Me! is a six-set series of children's books about saints, including the holy people of the: *Saints of North America* who served our homeland; *Saints of Christmas*, who teach us to love Jesus; *Saints for Families*, who modeled God's love within and for the domestic Church; *Saints for Communities*, who served Jesus through various roles and professions; and *Saints for Sacraments*, who showed great love for the sacraments.

The eight books in *Saints of the Beatitudes* (a word meaning "a list of blessings from God") introduce nine holy people who exemplify attributes Jesus articulated in his Sermon on the Mount. Faustina Kowalska's diary *Divine Mercy in My Soul,* read by millions, helped spread God's message of mercy. Patrick, a missionary, brought Christianity to Ireland. Monica prayed her wayward son, Augustine, would return to the faith. He did and was canonized. Katharine Drexel abandoned her comfortable life to become a nun. Carlo Acutis shared his faith and love of the Eucharist through technology. Bernadette Soubirous experienced visions of the Blessed Virgin Mary. Pope John XXIII convoked the Second Vatican Council, hoping to revive the Church. Jude was an apostle of our Lord.

Which saint was captured by pirates and sold into slavery? Name the saints with back-to-back feast days (August 27–28). Who gave $20 million to build churches and schools? Who created a website about eucharistic miracles? Who did Jesus appear and speak to? Who said, "My job is to inform, not to convince"? Who wrote *Peace on Earth* in 1963? Who is the patron of impossible causes? Find out in the *Saints of the Beatitudes* set—part of the *Saints and Me!* series—and help children connect to the lives of the saints.

Introduce your children or students to *Saints and Me!* as they:

—**READ** about the lives of the saints and are inspired by their stories.

—**PRAY** to the saints for their intercession.

—**CELEBRATE** the saints and relate them to their lives.

Free activities for children to use with this book may be downloaded at Liguori.org.

The Beatitudes

Divine blessings Jesus names in his Sermon on the Mount

Matthew 5:3–12

Saints of the Beatitudes

Patrick
Blessed Are the Poor in Spirit (Verse 3)

Monica and Augustine
Blessed Are the Mournful (Verse 4)

Katharine Drexel
Blessed Are the Meek (Verse 5)

Carlo Acutis
Blessed Are the Righteous (Verse 6)

Faustina Kowalska
Blessed Are the Merciful (Verse 7)

Bernadette
Blessed Are the Pure of Heart (Verse 8)

Pope John XXIII
Blessed Are the Peacemakers (Verse 9)

Jude the Apostle
Blessed Are the Persecuted (Verses 10–12)

Saint Faustina Kowalska is a popular saint of the Catholic Church. She loved Jesus very much and trusted him with all her heart. Jesus asked her to tell people about his love and mercy.

She is called the Apostle of Mercy because she worked hard to spread Jesus' message of Divine Mercy.

Saint Faustina was born in Poland, the third-oldest of ten children. Her parents named her Helena. She was a beautiful baby!

Her family lived on a small farm. Everyone helped with the chores. They planted crops, and they fed the chickens and the pigs. Helena liked to help her mother in the kitchen. Her family prayed together every morning and every night.

Helena felt close to Jesus when she prayed. She loved Jesus so much that she wanted to become a nun. One night she told her parents that Jesus wanted her to join the convent.

Her father got a serious look on his face. He thought a moment, gave her a hug, and said, “Helena, you are so young. Let’s talk about this when you are older.”

Helena was sad, but she obeyed her parents. She went to school, did her chores, and prayed every day. Jesus was always on her mind and in her heart.

When she was sixteen, she got a job as a housekeeper. A few years later, she decided it was time to join the convent.

1

She took a train to Warsaw, a large city in Poland. Helena went to Mass at Saint James Church. “God, please help me,” she prayed.

She walked from one convent to another, knocking on each door. "I would like to become a nun," Helena begged. She was turned away many times, and it seemed like no one wanted her.

Finally, the Mother Superior for the Congregation of the Sisters of Our Lady of Mercy invited her inside their convent. "Come in, dear child," she said with a smile.

Helena was twenty years old when she received her habit and took the name Sister Maria Faustina of the Blessed Sacrament. Through daily prayer, she grew very close to Jesus. Two years later, she took her first vows.

Sister Faustina was kind, helpful, and she worked hard. She traveled to the other convents of the order and helped in the kitchen as a cook. Sister Faustina also greeted visitors at the front door. She liked to work in the garden with the other nuns. *"Oh, I am so happy! Thank you, Jesus!"* she thought to herself.

One night while praying alone in her room, something wonderful happened! The room suddenly filled with light. She saw Jesus standing before her in a white robe. He held up his right hand to bless her and touched his heart with his left hand. Red and white rays flowed from his heart. Sister Faustina was a little scared, but she was very happy at the same time.

Jesus said to her, “I want you to paint a picture of me. Put the words, ‘Jesus, I trust in You’ on the bottom of the painting.”

Then Jesus asked her to write down everything he told her in a diary. He wanted people to know how much He loved them. His special message for all people would be called "Divine Mercy." Sister Faustina was happy to help Jesus.

After taking her final vows, she met Father Michael Sopocko. He became her spiritual director. "Oh, Father, I have so much to tell you," Sister Faustina said. After hearing the amazing story about Jesus, he sent her to talk to a special doctor. "Do not worry. Sister Faustina is telling the truth, I'm sure of it," the doctor said. Father Sopocko told Sister Faustina, "I will help you spread the message of Divine Mercy."

Father Sopocko was a good priest. He helped Sister Faustina. He talked to her when she was worried. "Keep a diary like Jesus told you," he said. She did! He found an artist to paint the picture of Jesus.

Jesus appeared to Sister Faustina a lot. He taught her the Chaplet of Divine Mercy and the prayer at the Hour of Mercy. He said he wanted people to celebrate his love and mercy on a special day. Sister Faustina wrote Jesus' words in her diary and hoped people would read it and learn about Jesus and his Divine Mercy.

Sadly, Sister Faustina got very ill. During her time in a hospital and after she died, the message of Jesus' love and mercy for all people spread.

Pope Saint John Paul II knew all of this. He canonized Sister Faustina on April 30, 2000. He announced that the first Sunday after Easter would be called Divine Mercy Sunday. Everywhere, Catholics rejoiced!

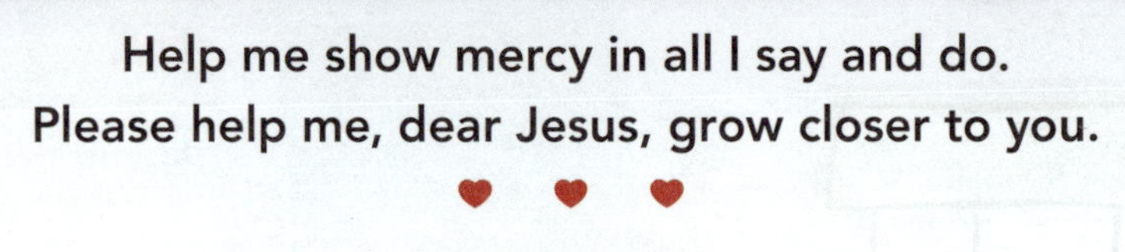

Help me show mercy in all I say and do.
Please help me, dear Jesus, grow closer to you.

Saint Faustina,
Your heart was full of love for Jesus.
You helped Jesus spread his message
of love and mercy.
Help me share his love and mercy with others
by my words and actions.
Help me to always trust in Jesus. Amen.

GLOSSARY (NEW WORDS)

Apostle: A person who is sent out to others with an important message

Beatitudes: A list of blessings from God

Canonize: The pope declaring that a person is a saint in heaven

Chaplet of Divine Mercy: A prayer Jesus taught Saint Faustina using the beads of the rosary

Congregation of the Sisters of Our Lady of Mercy: A group of women religious; they carry on Saint Faustina's mission of sharing God's mercy.

Convent: Where a group of women religious live

Diary: A book of written notes about a person's experiences and thoughts

Divine Mercy: God's great love for all people

Habit: Clothing worn by members of religious orders

Hour of Mercy Prayer: A special prayer Jesus taught Saint Faustina that is said at 3 PM, the hour Jesus died on the cross

Mercy: Care and love of others, especially someone who is hurting or troubled

Mother Superior: Leader of a group of women religious

Spiritual Director: One who guides people in their faith

Vow: A special promise, especially one made to God